Wandering Woman: Washington

The Ultimate Road Trip: One Woman's Journey Across the United States by Car

Julie Bettendorf

Contents

Introduction

"Not all who wander are lost."

Are you sure? I thought to myself, as I tried not to panic. I was a long way from anything familiar, but that was how it should be. I had driven thousands of miles on dusty, pothole-filled roads. It's often on the worst roads that you can discover something truly amazing.

My dusty CRV was parked beside me, containing one restless dog and a variety of snack bags, all empty by now. There were no buildings in sight, no cars or people or movement at all. Only the constant humming of the insects as they buzzed around my head.

I turned to my left – another straight road that trailed off into the distance. I glanced over to the right, then behind me – two more barely discernible roads stretched out into the abyss. I was in a four-way intersection with no signs, no sense of direction, and no sign of life for several miles. No cell service either. *Damn*, I thought. *I'm lost.*

How did I get here? I couldn't help but feel like this little intersection was a cruel metaphor for life. I began to daydream, imagining each road might transport me back to a different time, a different role in my life, and a different me.

If I took the road from whence I came, it could lead me all the way back to Oregon, back to my cheating third husband, back to a life of loneliness and solitude. There is no greater loneliness than being married to someone who isn't actually present in your life.

If I took the road to my left, perhaps it could take me back to my career as a dental hygienist, a job I hated deep down in my soul. There is something so disengaging about cleaning teeth for a living. It's a disgusting, smelly way to get a paycheck. It pays well, which is great, but the best part is the huge gob of friends I enjoy to this day.

Or maybe the road to my right, *yes – maybe that's the path*, I imagined. Maybe it could take me back to my real treasure, my kids. Back to their smiling, innocent faces as toddlers, as they danced around the Christmas tree and their father and I were still married. Back when they still needed me for every little thing.

But, that was just it. I didn't feel needed anymore. My kids weren't toddlers anymore – they were both full-grown adults, and far too busy for me. My dental buddies were still working, but I wasn't. Dental hygiene had robbed me of the cartilage in my fingers, giving me severe, disabling arthritis. And, I wouldn't be returning to any more husbands either, because three marriages were quite enough for me.

All three of these paths, all three of these roles – the wife, the mother, and the dental hygienist – had seemingly been stripped from me within a year. I was lost and looking to find myself again.

The funny thing about this phrase, "not all who wander are lost" – is that, in my experience, wandering and being lost walk hand-in-hand with one another, and the expression can be flipped. In my experience, not all who are lost are wandering, and that is a real disservice to the beauty and clarity that the world has to offer.

When one becomes lost, wandering is the only option to guide oneself back to a path. After all, one could not come upon any dirt path at all without wandering.

I began wandering at an early age, both with my mind and with my feet. At eight years old, I was reading a book about archaeology and dreaming of one day seeing Egypt. I didn't follow a traditional path in high school either, going heavily into foreign languages, in hopes of one day using them.

At twenty-five years old, I divorced my first husband (the dental student who talked me into becoming a dental hygienist so I could work for him) and decided to give traveling a real shot. I took off for the Andes and Macchu Picchu, climbing up ancient Inca stone steps to reach the magnificent ruins.

Anyone who has been to Macchu Picchu will tell you there is something ethereal and deeply spiritual about the place. The ruins stretch out across the emerald green mountains, way up in the middle of the sky. Macchu Picchu gave me my first experience of feeling history. This trip inspired me to come back and complete a degree in archaeology, and I've been wandering ever since.

More travel followed including a backpack trip around Europe for three months, by myself, and trips to Britain, Italy, and Greece. I visited the burial places of Crusaders, mummies, and ancient kings. I happened upon the castle of my namesake in Bettendorf, Luxembourg, and wandered my way through European history.

My favorite excursion by far was finally seeing Egypt with my daughter in 2012. Just like my childhood dream envisioned, I rode a camel beneath the pyramids of Giza, with my head wrapped in some man's sweaty turban. It was perfect.

Traveling has always been my own personal antidote to pain. I went to Mexico after my first and second divorces, Canada after my third, and Italy after my dad died. Call it avoidance if you want, but I call it an accelerated form of healing in the purest sense of the word. I believe travel can heal your soul.

Wandering has always worked its wonders on me – made me feel renewed, rejoiceful, grateful, and purposeful. It's been my medicine.

So, as I stood in that intersection, I once again wondered how wandering had led me so astray this time. *What the hell am I supposed to do now?* It was then that I realized that one last path had not been considered yet – the path which stretched straight out in front of me. *Which role does this represent?* I pondered.

The answer smacked me in the face.

That last dirt road – the only path that could take me where I wanted to go, the only path that ever truly healed me or showed me the way – was the path of the traveler. The wife, the mother, and the hygienist roles – though valued in their time – were sitting in the bleachers now. It was time to welcome and enable my boldest, bravest, and perhaps most pivotal role yet:

The role of the Wandering Woman.

Welcome to Wandering Woman

T his book is for you – the grieving empty nester mom, the be-
grudged housewife, the woman in need of a drastic change in
her life. Really, this book is for anyone with a passion for traveling.
If you feel lost with no sense of direction or purpose in life, that's a
bonus – this book will be even more appealing to you. And lastly, if
you're a man reading this book, congratulations for holding a book
with the word woman in the title. You're contributing to gender
equality, and that's pretty neat.

I decided to combine three of my dearest loves – travel, history, and archaeology – and put them into a book because I believe wandering has the power to change your life. I have been to many areas of the world and had too many outstanding experiences to list. However, by the time both my children had moved out in 2017, I had never seen my

Me

own country – America. It was the perfect time to explore a new country (my own) and discover a new me at the same time.

So, I packed up my Honda CRV, along with some gear and my 14-year-old furry friend, Sadie. Wandering Woman is the chronicle of my journey across eleven states, discovering the joy of getting lost and finding myself along the way.

Why America?

A *merica, the beautiful?* I sure think so, but I didn't realize just how beautiful our country is until I embarked on traveling across eleven western states in a year.

The United States offers everything for the discerning palate. From spectacular beaches, austere mountains, to rolling plains, our country has it all. It's difficult to comprehend just how large and impressive our scenery is, until you experience it first-hand, with the ultimate road trip.

I also realized just how much of our history is missing from U.S. history I was taught as a kid. The history of our country didn't begin with the pilgrims landing on Plymouth Rock in the 1600s. Our history is far more ancient, with rock art and archaeological sites dating back over 12,000 years.

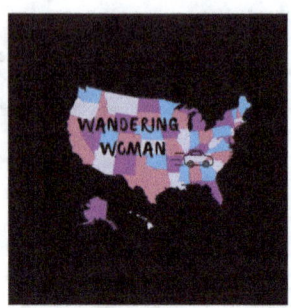

We also owe a tremendous debt to early pioneers who tamed our land. The Mormons and other groups ventured into the great unknown with their families and their worldly possessions. Some of them pulled cumbersome handcarts across the country to settle in inhospitable, dangerous locations.

The goal of Wandering Woman is to bring history back to life and make it interesting again. I am presenting some famous sites, and many little-known ones. You will take the road-less-traveled with me, while we explore ghost towns, rock art sites, archaeological sites, and museums, to discover the colorful tapestry that is our country.

I present some history, including dates, but my goal is to present more of the real-life stories of history, including ghost stories, profiles in history, voices from the past, and moments in time, to give you, the reader, a deeper understanding of the context of history.

This is by no means an exhaustive list of places to visit. In fact, I encourage you to discover America for yourself, as I did, by making a trek across the land by car. You can explore as the early explorers did, just a little more comfortably, with a lot less hardship.

I hope you enjoy this book and take a little time out to discover our beautiful country, and maybe even discover yourself in the process.

Safe Travels,

Julie Bettendorf

Welcome to Washington

The Evergreen State

*W**ashington*** has an unearthly beauty about it, from the craggy, windswept coastline in the west to the golden fields in the east. Washingtonians are proud of their state, as they should be. People are warm, friendly, and anxious to show you the beauty of where they live. Visit Washington, and you may not want to leave.

5 things to love about Washington:

Victorian era towns like Port Townsend

The elegant cityscapes of Seattle

The spectacular, rugged coastal scenery

The proud military history in Fort Walla Walla and Fort Worden

Quaint, charming historic towns like Oysterville

Dreams of Washington

"Earth does not belong to us; we belong to the earth. Take only memories, leave nothing but footprints."–**Chief Seattle**

"For generations, people have come to U.S. shores to seek opportunity. It's what my grandfather did a century ago, when he came to Seattle, and worked as a houseboy just one mile from the Washington State governor's mansion that I was privileged to inhabit for eight years."–**Gary Locke**

"Washington is nicknamed "The Evergreen State" because it sounds better than "The Incessant Nagging Drizzle State.""–**Dave Barry**

Top Stuff to See in Washington

Favorite Washington Historical Sites:

- Whitman Mission
- Frenchtown

Favorite Washington Towns:

- Port Townsend
- Oysterville

Favorite Washington Museums:

- Karpeles Manuscript Library Museum, Tacoma, Washington
- Fort Walla Walla Museum

Favorite Washington Scenic Drives:

- State Route 410 through Rainier National Forest
- Highway 101 around the Olympic Peninsula

When driving through Washington, be on the lookout for:

Elk and deer, sometimes in the middle of the road

Early Washington

Early Port Townsend

Early Washington Logging

Early Frenchtown Church

Western
Washington

Port Townsend, Washington

Port Townsend

B eautiful ***Port Townsend*** redefines picturesque. The stately Victorian buildings along the waterfront give you a feeling of stepping back in time.

The town was named by Captain Vancouver in 1792, to honor his friend, the Marquis of Townshend. Finch

The town was founded in 1851 by Alfred Plummer, an early homesteader. It became a US customs port in 1854, and by 1880, 1000 ships from all over the world came through Port Townsend. Jefferson County Historical Society

When you are in Port Townsend, pay a visit to the **Kelly Art Deco Light Museum**.

It's a fascinating place, chock full of antique light fixtures and innumerable treasures.

My favorite pieces in the museum are the sedan chairs, one from 1700s France, and the other from 1800s China. Kelly Art Deco Light Museum

Another great way to spend a few hours is at the *Jefferson Museum of Art and History*, housed in the old courthouse.

It contains a fascinating collection of logging history, seafaring, transportation, and other topics all wonderfully presented.

The museum also contains some excellent historical photos for you to enjoy.

My favorite section of the museum is the basement, which houses the old jail. You can see the "old ball-and-chain" and the feeding door, through which meals were shoved.

Another area of Port Townsend, not to be missed, is *Fort Worden*. The fort was built in 1896 to defend the naval installations of Puget Sound.

It's named after Navy Admiral John Worden, commander of the USS Monitor during the Civil War. The army left Fort Worden in 1953.

Fort Worden contains four 3-inch guns, two 5-inch guns, eight 6-inch guns, seven 10-inch guns, four 12-inch guns, and sixteen 12-inch mortars. A 12-inch mortar weighed 12,000 pounds and could fire 700 pound ammunition up to a distance of 9 miles. Fort Worden

The oldest building on the grounds of Fort Worden is Alexander's Castle, a medieval looking tower structure built in 1892. Alexander built it as a honeymoon present for his bride, back in Scotland. When he went back to Scotland to retrieve her, she had married another man.

You can complete your tour of Port Townsend with the ***Point Wilson Lighthouse***. The lighthouse was built in 1879 to guide ships through the Admiralty Inlet that connects the Strait of Juan de Fuca to Puget Sound.

Point Wilson itself was discovered by Captain George Vancouver in 1792 and named after his friend, Captain George Wilson. It's a beautiful, serene spot. Point Wilson

How to get to Port Townsend attractions:

The Kelly Art Deco Light Museum is located at 2000 W. Sims Way

The Jefferson Museum of Art and History is located at 540 Water Street

Fort Worden is located at 200 Battery Way

Point Wilson Lighthouse is located at 200 Battery Way East

Ghost Story:

Point Wilson Lighthouse is home to the ghost of a woman wearing a long gown, who wanders the grounds around the lighthouse.

The ghost is believed to be that of a mother whose daughter was lost back in 1920, when two vessels collided with each other near the lighthouse. Six people died in the wreckage, including the poor daughter. The mother searches for her lost daughter still.

A word about Victorian life:

Early Port Townsend conformed to Victorian ideals, but also had its share of crime and vice. There were two areas of town. Uptown Port Townsend, where citizens visited each other via calling cards, when a person was "at home." They built magnificent mansions, played tennis, held yacht races, went to the theatre, and rode bicycles.

Downtown Port Townsend was where the money was made to build the magnificent mansions and enjoy a lavish lifestyle. Downtown employment and recreation involved drinking, gambling, brothels, and betting on horses. Shanghaiing sailors was also a lucrative way to make a living in Port Townsend. Jefferson County Historical Society

Profiles in history:

Max Levy, "the king of crimpers" was a Port Townsend resident, famous for shanghaiing men and making money from it. He was hard at work from the 1890s to 1910 supplying unwitting men to ships leaving port. He worked out of a boardinghouse near the wharf, where he had easy access to sailors.

Levy employed men known as "runners" who would select victims, wait until they were drunk and dumped them in a waiting ship. When the men woke up, they were already out to sea. Indians were never selected because Levy didn't want the Bureau of Indian Affairs to come investigate, and local residents were exempt too. Shanghaied men were usually loggers, soldiers, drifters, or farmers.

Sea captains paid Levy for each man he was able to deliver. He finally stopped when shanghaiing was outlawed in 1910. Levy was never convicted of committing a crime. He died in San Francisco in 1931.

The 1000 Year-Old Tree

O n a road trip, you never know what is around the next corner. I stopped at a rest area just before you cross the border into Canada and was greeted by an amazing, massive tree stump. This western red cedar tree *IS* history. It's over 1000 years old, has a diameter over 20 feet, and was once 200 feet tall.

In 1893, the stump died from a fire that started in its base. In 1916, the archway through the trunk was cut, and in 1922 the stump was moved by horse teams 150 yards north of its original location. In 1939, it was taken apart and pieced back together alongside Hwy 99. Finally, in 1971, the tree was moved to its current location.

How to get to the 1000 Year-Old tree:

The 1000-year-old tree is located at the Northbound Smokey Point Rest Stop near Arlington, Washington.

A word about dendrochronology:

Dendrochronology is the study of tree rings, to find out the age of wood. It's a useful technique for archaeologists, climatologists, and other scientific disciplines. A core sample is taken from a piece of wood and compared against other samples in the same geographic location, which have known dates. When the tree rings match, the date of the wood can be determined.

Tree rings provide a record of catastrophic events too, including forest fires, droughts, earthquakes, and insect infestations. Typically, a year of growth is equal to one tree ring. During a period of wet climate, the tree ring will be wide, and during a dry climate, the tree ring will be narrower.

Dendrochronology can help determine the age of wooden buildings, wood beams which were cut as posts for other building materials, and many other aspects of history and archaeology. Dendrochronology also determined the age of the 1000-year-old tree in Washington State.

Seattle

S eattle is a beautiful city, with its bustling waterfront, to its
many museums, there is something for everyone. When you

visit Seattle, you must see the **Pike Place Market**, a famous landmark dating from 1907.

The market was begun as a reme-
dy to price fixing, giving the public a way to obtain cheap food.

The market has everything you
would ever want to buy including fresh seafood, produce, fresh
flowers, and just about everything
else.

I visited the **Klondike Gold
Rush Museum**. It's a good museum, with a lot of excellent recre-
ations of life "the way it was"
back in the gold rush times of the
1890s.

Seattle was a major supply spot and jump-off point for gold seekers on their way to the Yukon. My favorite items in the museum were the many historical photographs lining the walls. Klondike Gold Rush Museum

How to get to Seattle attractions:

The Pike Place Market is also located in downtown Seattle at 85 Pike Street.

The Klondike Gold Rush Museum is located in downtown Seattle at 319 Second Avenue South.

Profiles in history:

Chief Seattle was born around 1780, and he was able to see Captain George Vancouver exploring Puget Sound in 1792. During the influx of white settlers, Seattle was an advocate for peace, instead of war. He was instrumental in bringing about the Medicine Creek Treaty between the US and

Puget Sound tribes in 1854. He
died on June 7, 1866.

Voices from the past:

*"When the memory of my tribe
shall become a myth among white
men, when your children think
themselves alone in the field,
the store, the shop-they will not
be alone. When you think your
streets deserted, they will throng
with the returning hosts that once
filled and still love this land,
for the dead are not powerless."*
Chief Seattle, 1854.

Ghost story:

Chief Seattle's daughter, Kikisoblu, known also as Princess Angeline by early Seattle residents, lived at the foot of Pike Street. She sold baskets and did laundry to support herself. She died at age 85 on May 31, 1896. Her ghost has been seen on the lower levels of the market, close to where she used to live. She is a slow moving figure, using a cane, and wears a red kerchief on her head. Mayo

Tacoma

T**acoma* is home to the ***Karpeles Manuscript Library Museum, a fascinating place with a fabulous collection of documents.

It's a free museum containing original written manuscripts including a letter from Henry VIII attesting to his right to rule France,
dated 20 March, 1517.

Another document from history
is a letter from Elizabeth I, written in 1587, about her campaign
against the Spanish Armada.

One of my favorites is an account of the Titanic rescue by
the captain of the Carpathia,
Arthur Henry Rostrow.

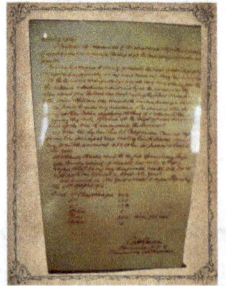

The account is dated April 27,
1912 and is in 2 pages.

The manuscript museum also has rotating exhibits, and when I visited, the exhibition was original manuscripts authored by Charles Darwin. 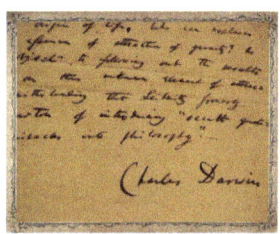 Karpeles Manuscript Library Museum

 The curator of the museum told me exhibits change every 4 months, and that I just missed the exhibit of major ideas in medicine, which I would have loved to see. Go see this museum in Tacoma. It is a wonderful collection of written history.

How to get to Karpeles Manuscript Library Museum:

The Karpeles Manuscript Library Museum is located in Tacoma, Washington at 407 South G Street.

Puyallup

P**uyallup, Washington* is the site of the ***Meeker Mansion, home to pioneers Ezra and Eliza Jane Meeker. Ezra Meeker is known as the "Father of the Oregon Trail" and was instrumental in marking out the entire trail from Missouri to Oregon, so the trail wouldn't be lost to history.

The Meeker Mansion is a 17-room, 10,000 square foot Victorian mansion, completed in 1890.

Each of the rooms is built using a different type of wood.

The mansion has 2 bathrooms, each with hot and cold running water.

There are 6 fireplaces in the Meeker Mansion, beautifully finished in tile.

The Meeker Mansion is furnished with all the luxuries of the time. It's full of wonderful original stained glass windows.

My favorite room of the house is the drawing room, complete with a spectacular grand piano.

One unusual feature are the "speaking tubes" a system of inter-connecting tubes within the walls of the house. Family could talk to people in other rooms without yelling.

The Meeker Mansion contains many artifacts which were carried across the Oregon Trail. One of my favorites is the handkerchief doll, made out of a family member's handkerchief.

Another favorite is the patchwork quilt, often made using clothing from family members left behind, as a remembrance of them. This quilt was brought to Washington in 1881.

How to get to Meeker Mansion:

The Meeker Mansion is located at 312 Spring Street, in Puyallup, Washington

Profiles in history:

Ezra Meeker took his first trip over the Oregon Trail when he was 22 years old, and his last trip was a fly-over when he was 94. Ezra left Indiana in 1852, with his wife Eliza, their 7 week old son, and Ezra's brother. They wished to join the wagons headed west to Oregon. The trip to Portland would take the group 5 months. Ezra lost 20 pounds by the end of the trip, and had to carry Eliza up the banks of the Willamette River. They arrived in Portland with $2.75 to make a life with.

Ezra became wealthy farming hops, used to flavor malt liquors. He became famous and he and Eliza were received by Victoria, the Queen of England. He built an impressive Victorian mansion in Puyallup, Washington, the town they called home.

Ezra couldn't forget the Oregon Trail, so at 76, he traveled by ox-drawn wagon back over the Oregon Trail, this time in reverse. He traveled with his dog, his driver, and his two oxen on a trip that would take 11 months. As he traveled, he spoke of preserving the Oregon Trail. He met with President Theodore Roosevelt to ask for funding of the Oregon Trail Preservation Project.

In 1910, when he was 80 years old, he again went over the Oregon Trail to mark historical spots along the trail. This trip would take 2 years. In 1916, when he was 86, he traveled the trail again, this time to visit the Senate. He wanted the trail to be designated a military highway.

His last trip was made in an airplane, at the age of 94. This trip took 4 hours, compared to his original trip of 5 months. He met with President Calvin Coolidge and persuaded Congress to mint 6 million 50 cent Oregon Trail Memorial silver coins. 50 years after Ezra died, in 1978, the Oregon National Historic Trail was designated, thanks to the efforts of Ezra Meeker. Wagner

---

Voices from the past:

"...A might army of pioneers went West...this army made an unbroken column five hundred miles long." **Ezra Meeker**

"I longed to go back over the old Oregon Trail and mark it for all time for the children of the pioneers who blazed it, and for the world." **Ezra Meeker on speaking in schools about the importance of the Oregon Trail.**

A word about Victorian table manners:

During the time of the Meekers, etiquette and manners were of the utmost importance, especially table manners.

Rules to be Observed:

- Sit upright, neither too close nor too far away from the table

- Open and spread upon your lap or breast a napkin, if one is provided—otherwise a handkerchief

- Do not be in haste; compose yourself; put your mind into a pleasant condition, and resolve to eat slowly

- Keep the hands from the table until your time comes to be served. It is rude to take a knife and fork in hand and commence drumming on the table while you are waiting

- Taking ample time in eating will give you better health, greater wealth, longer life and more happiness ^{Meeker Man-sion Museum}

Southwestern Washington

Fort Columbia, Washington

Fort Columbia

F ort Columbia, Washington began its history when American Captain Robert Gray discovered the Columbia River near here in 1792. He was soon followed by British Captain George Vancouver a few months later.

American and English fur traders began frequently visiting the mouth of the Columbia soon after. The first permanent settlers came here in 1843. Due to its strategic location, Fort Columbia served to guard the mouth of the Columbia River, beginning in 1896.

The fort served as an important landmark up until the end of World War II. Fort Columbia was like a small town, with its own hospital, theater, and a jail.

The self-sufficient soldiers took on additional duties including gardening, baking, cooking, and other tasks to keep the fort running. Fort Columbia

How to get to Fort Columbia, Washington:

Fort Columbia is located at Chinook Point, in Chinook, Washington at the mouth of the Columbia River.

A word about the Northwest Passage:

The search for the Northwest Passage began with a dream of finding a sea route which connects the Atlantic and Pacific oceans. The purpose was to improve ease of trading between Europe and Asia. Great Britain, the United States, Russia, and Spain all searched for the route. Among the highlights:

- In 499 AD, a Buddhist monk traveled 10,000 miles from China to reach a coastline. Could this have been the Pacific Coast?

- In 1707, a Spanish ship wrecked off of the Oregon Coast

- In 1775, Spanish explorers land on the coasts of Washington and Oregon, claiming land

- In 1790, the British and Spanish lay claim to settle in the Northwest

- In May, 1792, Captain Robert Gray reaches and explores the Columbia River

- In October, 1792, Captain George Vancouver reaches and explores the Columbia River up to the mouth of the Willamette River Fort Columbia

Oysterville

*O*ysterville, Washington, is a beautiful little historic town on the Washington coast, established in 1854. It was named after the bountiful oyster beds nearby. When you visit, the stars of the show are the many historic, beautiful homes from the 1800s that line the main street.

The wonderful thing about Oysterville is that there are plaques in front of each of the historic homes, telling when the home was built, and who lived there.

One charming *cottage* was built in 1873 for Charles Nelson Sr. It once housed 7 children in just three rooms.

Also among the more interesting stories is that of the 1874 *Ned Osborne House*. The house was built for Ned's future wife, but unfortunately, she died before they could be married. Ned lived the rest of his life in the house, a bachelor to the end.

There is also a rustic *school-house,* built in 1907, and a serene *pioneer cemetery,* established in 1858.

One of the more memorable grave markers is that of two unknown sailors, over which a small sign reads "And the Sea Gave Up the Dead...REV 20:13.

How to get to Oysterville, Washington:

Oysterville is located on the Long Beach Peninsula north on Hwy 103 until you reach Oysterville Road.

Ghost Story:

Oysterville has more than one ghost story centered around the cemetery, which is said to sit on top of a Native American burial ground.

There are several drowning victims buried in the cemetery. Visitors complain of cold spots and a strange energy they feel.

The schoolhouse is another haunted place in Oysterville. The ghost of a young child who died during an epileptic seizure is said to haunt the building.

A word about sailor superstitions:

The rough, lonely life at sea was the perfect breeding ground for superstitions about doom and death. These are just a few of the many superstitions of the sea:

- Sailing on Friday was unlucky, because Jesus was crucified on a Friday

- Red hair, crossed-eyes, or flat feet was bad luck

- Flowers were said to bring bad luck, so they would be thrown overboard

- Killing a seagull or dolphin would bring bad luck

- Bare-breasted women were believed to calm the sea, which is why figureheads are often bare-breasted [Kitmacher]

Vancouver

T he city of ***Vancouver*** was named for Captain George Vancouver, of the British Royal Navy. He explored the Pacific
Northwest area from 1791 through 1795.

Fort Vancouver is a major national landmark within the city. Fort Vancouver opened in 1825 and was part of the Hudson's Bay Company's fur trading empire. John McLoughlin was the chief factor for the fort, and shared supplies with travelers on the Oregon Trail in the 1830s.

The military structures were built in 1849, and include an *officer's row* of Victorian mansions. The mansions are stately, especially the majestic *Marshall House*, built in 1886.

There are extensive *buildings, barracks*, and a *parade ground*, which make up the military part of Fort Vancouver.

Inside the *Visitor's Center*, you can enjoy a few wonderful artifacts including decorative pipes.

My favorite includes a Bavarian-made water pipe which may have belonged to a German-American soldier stationed at the Fort.

Another favorite are the president pipes, with the faces of Zachary Taylor and Millard Fillmore, the 12th and 13th presidents.

A short distance from the Visitor's Center, you can enjoy a superb *reconstruction of the original Fort Vancouver*, as it appeared during its fur trading days.

The hub of the fort was the *Chief Factor's House*, known as the "Big House". The interior had all the comforts of the time.

Other buildings included the *blacksmith shop* and *kitchen*, with two massive brick fireplaces big enough to cook for an army.

My favorite building is the **Post Surgeon's House**, which housed the surgeon and his family.

This same building also served as the fort hospital .

How to get to Fort Vancouver:

Fort Vancouver is located at 1501 E. Evergreen Boulevard, in Vancouver, Washington.

Ghost story:

One of the buildings in officer's row, known as the Grant House, built in 1850, is reportedly haunted by the ghost of Alfred Sully, a lieutenant colonel who commanded the fort from 1874, until he died in 1879. Visitors to Grant House report hearing footsteps on the upper floor.

Near the Grant House is the Nelson House, said to have blood-like liquid running down the walls. Barrack 614 was once a hospital and psychiatric ward. Visitors to the barracks have heard screaming and laughing.

One ghost story with a historic basis concerns a pipe repair in the auditorium of the fort in 1982. During the repairs, workmen uncovered several human skeletons in the basement. After the discovery and for the next ten years, soldiers heard footsteps in the auditorium.

The bones were analyzed and found to be Native American, from the period of British occupation in the 1840s to 1850s. The Native Americans had worked and died at the fort and were buried with no markers. The bones were properly buried in the late 1990s with traditional  Native American ceremony. After the reburial, the ghostly manifestations stopped.

Southeastern Washington

Near Frenchtown

Fort Walla Walla

Fort Walla Walla was established in 1856. When I visited Fort Walla Walla, I began my tour with the *cemetery*.

It's an inspiring place, with so many gravestones, marking the graves of soldiers and Indians alike, who fought against each other during the Indian wars in the area. There are also many graves of small children, who died of diphtheria.

Fort Walla Walla has a tremendous amount of artifacts, contained in *five buildings*.

One of my favorite pieces is an example of "trench art" created by a soldier in 1917-1919. During their idle time in the trenches, soldiers would get creative with handy objects. This piece is a vase made from a shell casing.

Five buildings are filled with ex-hibits, including items brought over on the Oregon Trail and a soldier's bible, published in 1853.

My favorite is the ***Territorial Prison***, containing ball-and-chain ensembles and other prisoner garb.

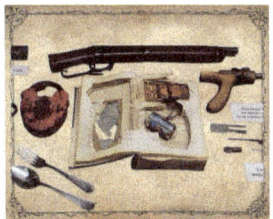

One of the most fascinating bits of history are the "book bombs" each of which has a mousetrap attached to a fuse, which is at-tached to a battery. The entire contraption is encased in a hol-lowed-out book. Fort Walla Walla

The real stars at Fort Walla Walla Museum are the ***pioneer buildings***, which were moved from various areas and reassembled on the grounds of Fort Walla Walla.

Among the buildings is a rustic log building which was once an old ***doctor's office***.

The inside contents are fascinating, including an examining table and other artifacts.

From the 1840s to the 1940s patients were anesthetized with ether or chloroform dripped on to a mask, which was often held by a family member.

The ***Prescott jail,*** built in 1903 is also fascinating.

A front door was sawed out after the building was completely built.

The ***Ransom Clark Cabin*** is another wonderful building, built 1n 1855. Ransom Clark was part of the surveying expedition led by John Fremont in 1843.

The cabin is cozily decorated with furnishings of the period.

Don't miss the ***Union School-house***, built in 1867 near Dixie, Washington.

The first through the eighth grades spent time in the school, with a class of about 15 to 18 students.

How to get to Fort Walla Walla, Washington:

Fort Walla Walla is located at 755 NE Myra Road, in Walla Walla, Washington.

Frenchtown

F ***renchtown*** is a small historical landmark near Walla Walla. It used to be a village of French-Canadian log cabins owned by members of the Hudson's Bay Company employees and their wives, most of whom were local Indian women.

Frenchtown was established around 1824, and has provided shelter for many famous faces, including Dr. John McLoughlin, Lewis and Clark, John C. Fremont, and Ulysses S. Grant.

All that remains today is a *log cabin* built in 1837 for an Indian leader, nicknamed "the Prince."
Frenchtown Historical Site

How to get to Frenchtown, Washington:

Frenchtown is located near Walla Walla at 8364 Old Highway 12.

A moment in time:

Today Frenchtown is a serene place, surrounded by fields of bright sunflowers. Back in December, 1855, it was once the scene of the longest Indian battle in Washington Territory history. It's known as the ***Battle of Walla Walla***, or the ***Battle of Frenchtown***. 350 Oregon Mounted Volunteers and 1000 Native Americans from the Walla

Walla, Palouse, Yakama, and Cayuse tribes fought against each other.

The battle was over tribal lands which were lost to the US government and settlers who began to populate the area which belonged to the Native Americans. The battle lasted four days, and supplies and ammunition began to run low on the side of the Volunteers. Reinforcements came on the fourth day, and the Indians withdrew from the battle.

Whitman Mission

The ***Whitman Mission***, near Walla Walla, was founded in 1836 by Methodist missionaries Marcus and Narcissa Whitman to teach the Cayuse and Umatilla Indians.

In 1847 the Whitmans were killed along with other family members and friends by the Cayuse Native Americans.

There are marked off sites where the mission and houses once stood.

The remains of the slain settlers are buried in a combined large grave. It is a beautiful spot, well worth visiting and a poignant reminder of the bravery of the early settlers.

The on-site ***museum*** contains some interesting artifacts including Narcissa Whitman's journal, written as she was traveling west. _{Whitman Mission}

One of my favorite pieces is a gorgeous timepiece.

How to get to Whitman Mission, Washington:

The Whitman Mission is located at 328 Whitman Mission Road, in Walla Walla, Washington.

A moment in time:

On an early morning in November, 1847, Marcus Whitman, who was a physician, was called to heal the sick during a measles epidemic. When he came out, he was hacked to pieces by the Indians.

Narcissa came out to help her husband, and she was shot in the face. An additional 13 other whites were slaughtered.

54 women and children were also kidnapped. Members of the Hudson's Bay Company paid the ransom to have them released, but several had already died.

Some believe that the Whitmans were murdered because Marcus Whitman failed to heal many of the Indians, who died of measles, cholera, and other diseases. It is also claimed that Joe Lewis, a half-breed, incited the Indians by saying that Dr. Whitman was poisoning them to obtain possession of their land. Whitman Mission

Voices from the past:

"At the time of the massacre, there were 72 people living at the mission, 42 of these were children. The day before the massacre, eleven of these were sick in bed. The Indians did not kill any of the girls, I have been told.

My grandfather was the only man to get through this terrible massacre alive." ***Margaret Osborn Mumford, granddaughter of a Whitman Massacre survivor, Josiah Osborn.***

Ghost story:

The ghosts of Marcus and Narcissa Whitman are said to appear on the mission grounds, next to the large stone marking the crypt containing their bodies.

Marcus and Narcissa appear just how they looked after the murders. Marcus appears soaked in blood, and Narcissa's face is unrecognizable from bullet wounds. They are seen most frequently during the early morning hours and then are said to fade away. Stansfield

Northeastern Washington

Chesaw, Washington

Molson

***M*olson**, Washington, has an interesting story. It was first
settled in 1900 by investor John Molson, and promoter
George Meacham. The town grew to a population of about 300

people and had a dentist, a lawyer, a newspaper, and a drugstore. A large three-story hotel known as the Tonasket was also built.

The town boomed again when the railroad came into town in 1905. Eight saloons and a mercantile store started up. Then came homesteader J.H. McDonald whose 160 acres contained 40 acres of downtown Molson, including the hotel. After several lawsuits, residents packed up and settled into New Molson. By 1906, New Molson and Old Molson were the same size.

A school was built in 1914 in between the two towns, and this area became Center Molson.
Weis

The remaining buildings of Molson include an *assayers office* from 1906, a *homestead cabin* from 1908, a *bank*, a *law office*, and the *first cabin* in Molson, built in 1898.

How to get to Molson, Washington:

Molson is located 2 miles south of the Canadian border, northeast of Oroville, Washington.

A word about preservation:

Many ghost towns are not restored. Instead, they undergo a process known as *"arrested decay."* The buildings are only repaired and stabilized to prevent them from collapsing, but they are not restored.

Efforts are made to stabilize rock foundations and repair leaking roofs to prevent further damage, but the buildings are left in their original condition at the time of purchase.

Chesaw

T he town of ***Chesaw*** is named after a Chinese man named Chee Saw who lived there with his Indian wife. It became a mining center in 1896 and contained a store, post office, assay office, multiple saloons, a three story hotel and several other log buildings. ^{Weis}

In 1900, Chesaw was also home to numerous millinery shops, selling all of the latest hats, clothing, and accessories.

Several people live in Chesaw today and there are a few ***original buildings*** remaining and a small ***pioneer cemetery***.

How to get to Chesaw, Washington:

Chesaw is 10 miles east of the Molson Junction.

A word about women's work:

Like their husbands, the wives of miners had an arduous life, a never-ending amount of toil. Women had to make meals from scratch, often growing their own vegetables, and raising their own protein. Since there was no refrigeration, they had to can or dry the food to preserve it. They also made their own bread.

Clothing was women's work as well, and most wives made clothing for the family, and then they had to keep the clothing clean. Laundry involved carrying the water and then heating it on the stove. Using soap they made themselves, miner's wives scrubbed garments and wrung them out before hanging them outside to dry.

A miner's wife kept the home clean by emptying chamber pots, and sweeping and scrubbing floors. Women also cared for ill family members since a doctor was often many miles away and unreachable.

Bodie

T he town of **Bodie** started up in 1896 when gold was found by
two prospectors. This tiny place originally had a restaurant,

livery, blacksmith shop, general store, and many homes. All of the buildings were made of logs.

Today you can see just a few **buildings** along the road, in various states of dilapidation. The two-story **Bodie school** is located on the other side of the street.

The upper level may have been an apartment used by the teacher, known as a **teacherage**. Weis

How to get to Bodie, Washington:

Bodie is 15 miles from the town of Wauconda, and about 12 miles south of the Canadian border.

Fun fact:

The Bodie gold mine was owned by several different people, including the Wrigley brothers, of chewing gum fame.

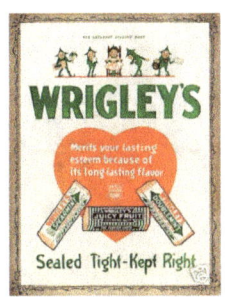

A word about mail order brides:

The aftermath of the Civil War and the movement West for the Gold Rush led to a scarcity of men in the Eastern United States. The hardships of living in mining camps and prospecting was not a great environment for women either, so there were too many men and too few women in the West.

Published numbers state the ratio was sometimes as great as 200 men to 1 woman. Business-minded people began what was known as the "mail-order bride" industry. A well-read newspaper known as the Matrimonial News listed advertisements for women seeking to marry men, and for men seeking to marry women.

Here are two of the more striking examples of ads from January 1887:

"A good looking young lady of 19, 5 feet 3 inches high, black hair and eyes, would like to find someone to love."

"I want to know some pretty girl of 17 to 20 years. I am 29, 5 feet 9 inches tall, a blonde: I can laugh for fifteen minutes and I want some pretty girl to laugh with me."

And from the New Plan Company Catalog, September 1917:

"Winsome Miss of 18 years, considered attractive looking, have many friends, very pleasant and lively, blue eyes, dark hair, fair complexion, good education, good cook and house-keeper, weight 130, height 5 feet; would make the right man a good wife; have a profit of $10,000; will answer all letters containing stamps."

"Would like to correspond with a farmer about 30 to 35 years old. Am an American widow of 33; height 5 feet, 2 inches; weight 200; brown eyes; brown hair; common school education. Personal property worth $1500. Object matrimony. No flirts need write." Enss

Republic

T he town of **Republic**, originally known as Eureka Gulch, was
founded by gold prospectors in the early 1900s. There is a
wonderful *Episcopal Church* built in 1909 and finished in 1910.

Right in town, you can dig up and keep a little piece of history for yourself. At the ***StoneRose Eocene Fossil Site***, you can pay a mere $10 and dig up your own 50 million year-old fossils. You can take 3 fossils home with you.

It's an outstanding adventure, staffed by some very knowledgeable, helpful people. I found 3 plant fossils including one with a fossilized fly in it. You may run into nice groups of students while you are up there.

How to get to Republic, Washington:

Republic is located in north central Washington, at the intersection of State Routes 20 and 21.

Favorite Places to Camp

*W*anapum State Park Campground is a lovely choice in Eastern Washington. Many of the 52 campsites have spectacular views of Wanapum Lake. All sites have power, and there are showers plus an area for picnics, and a beach area for swimming. To find out more visit *parks.wa.gov*

Curlew Lake State Park in Republic is a perfect spot to enjoy the StoneRose Fossil Site. There are over 80 campsites for tents, RVs, and everything in between. You can reserve a site by visiting the Washington parks website at *https://washington.goingtocamp.com*

Fort Worden State Park near Port Townsend is an excellent home base for exploring Port Townsend and neighboring areas. There are two campground areas, the beach campground with 50 sites, and the lower forest campground with 30 sites. You can reserve a spot by visiting the Washington parks website at *https://washington.goingtocamp.com*

Campgrounds in Mt. Rainier National Forest are abundant and offer majestic mountain and forest scenery. There are three campgrounds within Mt. Rainier National Park, and countless smaller Forest Service campgrounds as you travel along. To find out more visit *parks.wa.gov*

Random Thoughts

What History Means to Me

First, let me start by sharing with you my opinion of what history isn't. History is not a collection of random dates, names, and places for you to memorize. History is not a dry and uninteresting class you have to pass to graduate.

I believe history is a tangible thing. You can actually *feel* history in the places you go, and the sights you see. I remember walking up to the Acropolis in Athens. I looked down at the well-worn marble steps and wondered about how many ancient philosophers had climbed these very steps, thousands of years ago.

You don't have to go far away to experience the *feeling* of history. If you are lucky enough to live in an old house, you may experience history in your own surroundings. You might say to yourself, *"If only these walls could talk."*

During my travels across the United States, I *felt* history in many, many places. If you travel across the country like I did, you will *feel* the wonderful history of our beautiful country for yourself, and you will never be the same. You will discover what it means to be an American.

Why I did it and why you can too:

I decided to travel across the country by car because I wanted to rediscover America. When I first set out to explore the history of our country, I wanted to find out why America is the greatest country on earth, and what it means to be an American.

The politics of these United States was frightening at the time. Our country was polarized, almost beyond repair. Whether it was Democrats or Republicans, Conservatives, or Liberals, everyone was fighting.

I wanted to rediscover the joy of being an American. I wanted to rediscover our rich history, our unique and wonderful people, our tapestry of multicultural heritage, and our rich natural resources. I thought a road trip by car across eleven western states was a good place to start.

I have a degree in Archaeology, and a passion for all things archaeological. I love history, with a side love of paleontology. It is these three passions that I set my trip agenda around. I set out to discover the archaeological sites, history, and paleontological world of our country.

As I travel and write my books, I get asked all the time, especially by women, "What is it like to travel by yourself? Aren't you scared?" The truth is, I believe everyone should do what I did. It's a wonderful way to discover our country, and to rediscover yourself. The truth is, I'm scared not to travel. Traveling allows you to get to know yourself, in ways not possible when sitting on the couch watching TV.

We tend to spend a lot of our lives tuning out the world and our place within it. When you travel, you are quite literally forced to deal with your own thoughts, emotions, and feelings. You can discover yourself while traveling. You can come to understand what makes you who you are, and how you can perhaps become a better person. Above all, traveling gives you mental clarity to figure out how to live with intent. It's a way to guide your life, not just wait for things to happen.

Travel Tips & Stuff

What You Need to Know

How to get started:

P lanning your trip should be one of the most exciting things about it. You want to be spontaneous, but it is also very wise to plan your route, so you can take full advantage of all the time and miles you will invest.

First, decide your passions. If you love airplanes, trains, or old vehicles, plan your trip around that. If you love gardens or architecture, seek that out as the focus of your trip.

Next, read and research areas of the country that will let you enjoy what you are interested in.

Make a list by state and city or town, of what you want to see.

Take your handy road atlas and locate the areas on the pages.

Make a tentative route plan, so you have an idea of where you are going.

Travel tip: Avoid trying to plan your trip down to a schedule of days, hours, or minutes. On a road trip, it will be virtually impossible to know where you will be on any given day. If you adhere to a schedule, you are more likely to stress out, and less likely to actually enjoy yourself, which is the whole point.

What you need:

You need to bring along a sense of adventure and a curious mind. You need to ditch the idea of always being on a schedule, and live a little more spontaneously to thoroughly enjoy yourself. Things will happen as you travel, both good things and bad things, and you need to prepare your mind and your soul for day-to-day changes.

So much of our lives are planned out. Between growing up, going to school, finding a career, marriage, kids, or whatever, people have lost much of the ability to be spontaneous. But you must take spontaneity on the trip with you, because you may make detours along the way to see something really spectacular.

So, for the practical stuff you need:

A great vehicle-I have a Honda CRV which is fabulous. It's old, a 2004, fully paid for, and will go anywhere. I see humongous RVs on the road, towing a car behind, and all I can think of is, they can't go just anywhere. They are too big. Bad gas mileage, cumbersome to drive, slow, and not agile like my CRV. So, I encourage you, if you want to go car camping and be able to go on remote dirt roads, get an agile vehicle, and Hondas are great.

Travel tip: Don't be afraid to do some modifications to your vehicle. I took one of my back seats out. (after watching a YouTube video) I threw in a twin mattress, a bit of drapery, and some netting. I also put some of those little portable light switches on the inside. I jettisoned anything I hadn't used up to that point. Don't be afraid to get rid of unnecessary stuff.

An awesome camera that you know inside and out. I use a Nikon and it takes wonderful pictures. Don't skimp on a camera, and don't think a cellphone camera is all you need, because you want the best for your beautiful photos.

A hot plate warmer-this little item was indispensable. You need a converter for it so you can plug it in to the cigarette lighter. Place your food inside it, carton and all, and then plug it in. 30 minutes for thawed food, about an hour and a half for frozen food. Boom! You have a hot meal by the time you stop for the night!

Window shades-the best ones are magnetic so you just place them against your windows and they cling to them, obscuring the view inside your car.

Portable cooler with wheels-another indispensable item that works great and is easy to move around. I use those nifty blue frozen blocks in mine.

Portable air compressor-this little gem plugs into your cigarette lighter and will inflate your tires if you have a flat. Fortunately, I haven't had to use this yet.

Portable battery charger and power bank-mine comes with battery cables and the power bank, yet once inside the case, it is small enough to put in your glove compartment. This little item, unfortunately, I have had to use, and it saved me.

Portable generator-mine came with a small solar panel, so it can be charged with solar or electricity. It has a decent battery life and also doubles as a light for night-time.

All season clothing-you never know what different states will bring for weather, so take hot weather and cold weather clothes, and a fair amount of shoes appropriate for hiking, or walking, sandals, and slippers, which are nice at night. Also take along a pair of cheap rubber flip-flops to wear in the public showers you might go into.

Your own pillows-I like my own pillows, so I don't wake up with neck cramps, especially after sleeping in the car.

Sleeping bag and cozy blankets-you want to stay warm and layering is everything.

Warm hat, warm socks, and fuzzy jammies to keep you warm for cold nights sleeping in the car.

A great road atlas, and great guidebooks-get one that's easy to read, with great pictures. For a road atlas, just get one that is easy to read.

A word about photography:

Along with a great camera, you need to have a great eye. This is easier than it sounds once you have worked with your camera and are comfortable taking pictures with it. I am not a professional photographer, but I like my pictures and other people do too.

These are my tips for taking great pictures:

- Experiment with taking both horizontal and vertical shots.

- Don't always put the subject of the photo in the middle of the photograph.

- This one is important: pay attention to the foreground, and if possible, have something, a plant or whatever, in the foreground to help give the photo dimension and depth.

- This one is important too: turn around often to see the view you just came from. I do this quite often and some of my best pictures have resulted from when I turned around and took the shot.

You can also take a mental photo. Place an image in your mind that you can call upon later. Use all of your senses to see, hear, smell, and maybe even to taste, what is around you. You have the means to fully experience your surroundings, and that is very important to a traveler. When you take a mental photo, be sure to jot down quick little details about what you saw, heard, smelled, or tasted, so you can jog your memory later.

And last, but not least...don't be posing in front of everything, everywhere, to show that you actually went somewhere. Most people want to see themselves in your photo and be mentally transported there, but they can't if you are there already.

To camp or not to camp:

Car camping is great. I prefer it to sleeping on the cold, hard ground in a tent. I can lock the doors, put my window shades up and be cozy for the night.

That being said, for me there were some do's and don'ts about camp sites. Some people camp in a Walmart parking lot and feel safe. I do not. I believe that if you are in a busy area, you're more likely to be confronted by a nut job who may bother you. Nothing against Walmart.

Same goes for casino parking lots. Many people believe that if they are in a public place, there is less chance of someone bothering them. I don't share this belief. I believe you are safer parked out in the middle of nowhere in the dark. That same nut job who can find you in a parking lot is not about to go driving around on dirt roads to see if anyone is parked there. At least that's my belief. You may not share it, and that's fine. Park and camp wherever you feel safe.

I don't go for rest areas either because they have a track record of incidents happening to people in rest areas, especially women travelers.

So, where do I camp? In state or national campgrounds, wildlife sanctuaries, or off on a dirt road somewhere, usually out in the middle of nowhere.

There are definitely times when I stay in a motel. I use Hotels.com because I like their stay 10 nights, get 1 night free deal. So, I book a hotel or motel if:

- The weather is too hot or too cold, or too rainy

- I am in a city and plan to stay awhile

- I'm tired of camping, need a shower, or my body hurts

- I need to do laundry

A word about safety:

When you are a woman traveling alone, it's critical to keep a low profile. Don't tell people you are traveling alone, where you are staying, or any other personal information.

I don't go to bars or get drunk. I'm not preaching but you are on your own, in a city or town you've never been to, and you don't know anyone, so it's not the time to lose control of what you are doing. When you are in control, you are better able to decide which people you want to get to know better.

Travel tip: If you feel vulnerable traveling alone, that's OK. Vulnerability is part of passion, and traveling is a passionate thing to do. You can put one of those family stickers on your vehicle to indicate to others that you are not traveling alone, which can help you feel more secure.

Maintain your connections:

When you are traveling alone, there is a definite sense of disconnection. It feels almost like you are the only one in the world, traveling through space and time. That's why it's critical to keep your connections to loved ones active.

Be on Facebook while you are traveling. You may not have internet a lot of the time, or the internet will be poor. Consider paying to have your phone be a hotspot. It's a little bit of money per month, but it's worth it and has saved me from being without internet. I love the convenience of it, and you will too.

Plan your journey around visiting family members or friends you haven't seen for a long time, or people that are good friends. When you see people you know, it will ground you, so you can continue traveling.

Check in by phone with loved ones. They worry about you, and it's good for both of you to stay connected no matter where you are.

Consider traveling with a pet. I started my trip with my beloved 14-year-old sheltie named Sadie. She didn't make it to the end of the trip. I lost her to bladder cancer about four months in. My Sadie was special, and I will never forget my first traveling buddy.

It took me a solid year to decide on getting another dog. I poured over profiles of rescue dogs, looking for a little buddy I could take care of. Best Friends Animal Society in Kanab, Utah, had my perfect match. I now have Rosie, an 8 year-old sheltie that looks just like Sadie and has many of the same mannerisms. Life is good again.

I highly recommend Best Friends Animal Society if you are looking for a pet. They have 3000 acres and house up to 1600 animals at one time including dogs, cats, horses, pigs, and just about everything else. The dedicated people at Best Friends are wonderful both to you, and your potential pet.

Travel tip: One of the easiest and best ways I stay connected while traveling is to offer to take a photo for someone I don't know. Many couples, families, or singles would love to have more pictures of themselves traveling. It's an easy and quick way to have a connection with a fellow traveler, and it's good manners too.

Practical matters:

You need to have an address to send your mail to. Keep in touch with whomever is nice enough to do this for you.

You will also need to come back occasionally to register your car, vote, go to doctor visits, and take care of any other business. You can't leave it all behind, as tempting as that may be.

Bad things that happened:

Remember when I said you need to take spontaneity with you on your trip? Well, there were many times when I used my spontaneity skillset.

The government shutdown happened smack dab in the middle of my travels. That meant that all of the National Monuments were closed. I did a lot of driving and circling around.

I also did a lot of circling around trying to avoid natural disasters. I traveled through Paradise, California shortly before a massive fire happened there. I tried to travel through the area again but was pushed out by massive flooding. My latest event was camping in Canyonville, Oregon and waking up to flames creeping down the hillside. That was day one of the Canyonville fire.

Besides being driven out by natural disasters, sometimes I was driven out by rude people. Many times it was centered around my furry traveling companion. I believe there are really only two types of people, those who love animals and those who don't. When people see me walking my beautiful, sweet, elderly dog, they either come up and pet her, or they say something harsh.

One incident was a woman, a total stranger, who came up to me smiling down at Sadie and asked how old she was. I replied, "She is 13 and a half years old." The woman replied very curtly "She needs to be put down." Sadie was walking around, alert, and happy, and yet this woman wanted me to end her life because she was old.

Speaking of animals, several times I came very close to driving into an animal on the road. I can't stress enough how many times this will happen to you, and all I can say is, be alert at all times while you are driving. When you travel a lot of miles, you will get tired, so stop and smell the roses, and try not to drive at night.

Good things that happened:

One of the sheer joys of taking a road trip is the unpredictability of it. You never know what you will see. I am originally from Oregon, and bears are not a common sight. So, while driving high up in the Blue Mountains, I looked over and saw a bear! So exciting! He didn't stay for long, kind of shy, but so cute. I love animals, so to see the rich and wonderful amount of wildlife in our country gladdened my heart.

I met many great people on my trip, from all walks of life. They were a walking, talking advertisement for our beautiful country. I smiled at them, and they smiled back. We are all Americans, and we are all part of the human race. When you meet people across the country, you realize just how important it is to get to know your fellow citizens, and learn more about how they view the world and our country.

I have to give a special shout-out to the many dedicated people, often volunteers, who staff our state and national parks and monuments. They work tirelessly to ensure the health of our natural resources, and help travelers enjoy their visit. The same is true of the many people who staff the museums in small towns and large cities. They enjoy history, like I do, and it shows in their smiles.

Along with wonderful people, I have seen an America that is spectacularly beautiful, with open prairies, majestic mountains, and crystal clear rivers. I have seen a small fraction of the history of our country. I have seen the memorials to the brave people who shaped our country. I have fallen in love with America in a way that was not possible sitting in my living room. People ask me, "would I do it again?" The answer comes easily, "Yes, in a heartbeat."

Bibliography & Further Reading

Davis, Jefferson and Janine, *A Haunted Tour Guide to the Pacific Northwest*, Norsemen Ventures, 2010.

Enss, Chris. Object, *Matrimony: the Risky Business of Mail-Order Matchmaking on the Western Frontier.* Globe Pequot Press, 2013.

Enss, Chris. *Tales behind the Tombstones*. Morris Pub., 2007.

Enss, Chris. *The Doctor Wore Petticoats: Women Physicians of the Old West.* TwoDot, 2006.

Finch, etc. al.., Jackie. *Eyewitness Travel USA*. DK Publishing, 2017.

Fort Vancouver, National Park Service, 2019.

Fort Vancouver Hawaiians at Fort Vancouver, National Park Service, 2009.

Fort Walla Walla Museum, Fort Walla Walla Museum

Hill, William E. *The Oregon Trail, Yesterday and Today: a Brief History and Pictorial Journey along the Wagon Tracks of Pioneers*. Caxton Press, 2014.

Huntington Library, *Beautiful Science Ideas That Changed the World*.

Johnson, Mary E. Benson. *Reminiscences of Oregon Pioneers*. East Oregonian Pub. Co., 1937.

Jones, Landon Y. *The Essential Lewis and Clark*. HarperCollins Publishers, 2000.

Kitmacher, Ira Wesley, *Haunted Graveyard of the Pacific*, History Press, 2021.

Lewis and Clark National and State Historical Parks, National Park Service

Mayo, Matthew P. Haunted Old West: *Phantom Cowboys, Spirit-Filled Saloons, Mystical Mine Camps, and Spectral Indians*. Globe Pequot Press, 2012.

Meeker Mansion Museum Tour, Puyallup Historical Society

Oregon City Loop Guide, Wallowa Whitman National Forest

Peck, David J. *Or Perish in the Attempt: The Hardship and Medicine of the Lewis and Clark Expedition*. The History Press, 2002.

Port Townsend. Arcadia Pub., 2008.

Rutter, Michael. *Bedside Book of Bad Girls: Outlaw Women of the American West.* Farcountry Press, 2008.

Smith, B. *Ghost Stories of the Rocky Mountains*. Lone Pine Pub., 1999.

Stansfield, Charles A. *Haunted Washington: Ghosts and Strange Phenomena of the Evergreen State*. Stackpole Books, 2011.

Wagner, Tricia Martineau. *It Happened on the Oregon Trail: Remarkable Events That Shaped History*. GPP, 2014.

Weis, Norm. *Ghost Towns of the Northwest*. Caxton Printers, 2002.

Index
Referenced by Sections

B

Battle of Walla Walla–see Frenchtown

Battle of Frenchtown–see Frenchtown

Big House–see Vancouver

book bombs–see Fort Walla Walla

British Royal Navy–see Vancouver

C

Carpathia–see Tacoma

Chee Saw–see Chesaw

Chief Factor's House–see Vancouver

Chief Seattle–see Seattle

Columbia River–see Fort Columbia

Coolidge, President Calvin–see Puyallup

D

Darwin, Charles–see Tacoma

dendrochronology–see 1000-year-old-tree

diphtheria–see Fort Walla Walla

E

About the Author

Julie Bettendorf is a world traveler with a degree in archaeology and a background in history. She has traveled extensively throughout Egypt, Central America, South America, Europe, and the United Kingdom, visiting archaeological and historical sites all along the way.

Currently, Julie is traveling around the US visiting ghost towns, ancient rock art sites, and archaeological wonders as part of research for her ongoing historical travel series entitled Wandering Woman. Wandering Woman is a set of state-by-state guides, full of photographs, historical anecdotes, and unique tips to help other women travel and explore solo across the US by car. Julie enjoys writing freelance blogs, traveling frequently with her two adult children, and hiking outdoors with her faithful dog companion Rosie.

Also by Julie Bettendorf

Wandering Woman: Washington is the sixth book in the ***Wandering Woman Travel Series***. The first five books in the series including ***Montana***, ***Utah***, ***Nevada***, ***Colorado,*** and ***Oregon,*** are available in ebook and paperback.

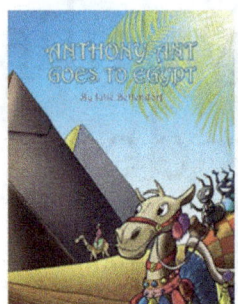 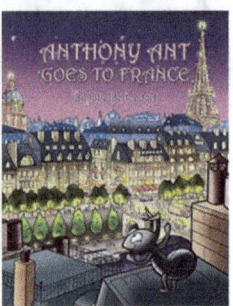

Julie has published two children's books in an ongoing, beautifully illustrated travel series entitled ***Anthony Ant Goes to France*** and ***Anthony Ant Goes to Egypt.***

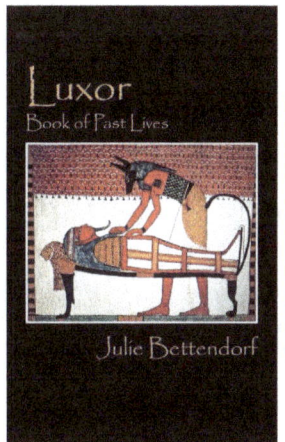

She has also published a work of historical fiction entitled ***Lux-or: Book of Past Lives*** which has recently been released as an audiobook, read by renowned narrator Barry Shannon.